LANE COUNTY JAIL — 1882-1959

Historic Building Lithographs by Eugene Artist, Joy Belle Jones

Front cover painting by Eugene Artist, Ellen Gabehart
Ellen has been involved with creating art her entire existence... "For me, where there is life, there is art—where there is art, there is life."

Watercolor graphics by Eugene Artist, Diane Burton
(Some of the graphics were converted to grayscale from original color paintings)
Diane started painting in her late fifties and... "it opened up a whole new world to me. It's a wonderful form of self expression."

Cover design and editing by C. Steven Blue of Arrowcloud Press
Page design and editing by Pat Edwards of *Groundwaters* Publishing, LLC

We extend our thanks to the additional panel members of the September 29th poetry event for helping C. Steven Blue in the selection process and the creation of this book. They are Deb Casey, Jennifer Chambers and Jon Labrousse.

Also, a big thank you goes to Scott Herron and the Eugene Public Library for their continued support in making these events possible.

Eugene
150th Birthday Celebration

Poetry Collection

Craft booth at the Saturday Market in Eugene, Oregon
www.flickr.com/photos/stuttermonkey/24799455/

Table of Contents

The Poems of

LANE COUNTY COURTHOUSE - 1898 - 1959

Oregon Dear Oregon

Oregon, dear Oregon, you're eternally in my blood,
Forever are you in my heart and soul.
From your rocky coastal ramparts, to your valley's fertile mud,
Up and o'er the mountains, to where your wheat fields roll.

I've shaded 'neath your canopies of virgin old-growth stands,
Roamed your lonely deserts where the ancient coyotes howl.
I've combed your windy beaches 'till my ears were numbed by sand,
Plied your nameless canyons, where the bear and cougar prowl.

I've scaled your lofty mountain tops, braved your endless snows,
Stood in awe and breathless at the splendors of your
    fall.
I've been lashed by the Columbia when the fierce
    gorge wind blows,
And heard the bull elk bugle, his timeless mating call.

From your pristine lakes aplenty, teeming brim with
    fish,
To your boundless wilderness, so rich in foul and game.
I've glutted on your bounty, you've granted every wish,
Oregon, dear Oregon, in my soul you've staked your
    claim.

~ Michael J. Barker

"Hoss" Barker is a former logger who, when he could no longer work in the woods, began writing poetry about logging and his experiences working with a bison herd. He later wound up at Paradise Lodge in the wild and scenic area of the Rogue River and spent six years there, mainly during the long, wet winters, writing four books of prose and poetry.

Peaceful Greens

...and sometimes,
when I lay in bed
in the late night quiet
of Oregon,

I can still hear the foghorn
of Venice Beach
amidst the slow tumble
of the early morning
marine layer.

The sounds of the lumber trains
are clear here;
long...
in the still night distance,
as I reminisce...
the lumbering waves
and walking along
the Marina del Rey jetty.
My life is different now:
cooler falls
and swooping morning birds,
rain-filled days
that break into clear blue
cloud-filled skies.

My surroundings are peaceful
 greens...
and fall's changing colours,
the sounds of tractors,
chain saws and squawking
Canadian geese flocks;
no longer the screaming motors
of freeways
and the constant sirens
of Los Angeles,
city of my lifetime,
long-gone city of angels.

Oregon is big,
like L.A.
but in a very different way.
Gone are the tall buildings, street
 lights
and 16 lane roads.
They have been replaced
by quaint farmhouses,
bright stars and gravel driveways.

Glorious evening fires
replace squabbling neighbors—
too close for comfort.
Sweatshirts, down vests
and cozy wool-blend socks
replace t-shirts, shorts
and flip-flops.

My wife hums and sings now.
She loves to ride
on a tractor lawn-mower.
Our neighbors bring us fresh produce:
tomatoes and cucumbers,
squash and raspberries,
lettuce, blueberries, apples and pears;
all grown in their own yards,
year-round... with joy.

Welcome to Eugene!
It is very different here!
As I ponder the trees,
the wind, the falling leaves,
the already greening grass
of fall's first rains...
the coolness of the air
is refreshing.

Our wrap-around porch
is truly a blessing,
for I can rock... or walk
without touching the rain,
while viewing it all,
all the splendor of fall...
and all the coming seasons

in Eugene,
in Oregon,
in the peaceful greens
of my new life.
It is very different here...

~ C. Steven Blue

After a 27-year career in stage production in Hollywood, CA, Steven is pursuing his lifetime calling as a lyrical/performance poet in Eugene, OR, where he also organized and hosted the 2012 Summer Reading Series Poetry Events for the Eugene Public Library. He has four published books and a blog on his website, www.wordsongs.com.

West Eugene Spring Starts

Morning dew's invisible
vapor escapes
the valley floor,
cows obligingly play
follow the leader,

billowing puffs of poo...f,
interrupting
multiple shades of blue
just west of town
on this exhilarating spring
morning, wrestle the fog
for the coastal range.

The smell hits me a quarter
mile before the turkey
vulture swoops
down to pick at the road kill—
another skunk for breakfast.

Newborn lambs,
devouring the fresh Emerald
Valley, pay no attention
to the airplane, also swooping;
aimed for Eugene's crackerjack
tarmac as gravel marks
my dusty road home
to a lane full
of bakin' and eggs.

Gangly canary daffodils,
the first sprouts of spring,
already corralling our front yard
trees, have been quickly followed
by bursting pink dogwoods.

Already evening
grosbeaks and yellow finches
gather, attracted
by chock-full feeders,
along with year-long hummers,
buzzing like giant bumblebees,
and jet plane swallows
zooming to catch
a mouthful.

Joel says...
"Welcome to Eugene—
just a little northwest
of Normal.
23 square miles
surrounded by reality!"

~ C. Steven Blue

Anything You Can Spare

It's hard to tell anymore
who's actually homeless
and who isn't but there
he was holding a spray
bottle and a stack of paper
napkins saying he'd either
wash my windshield or recite
one of his poems for any
part of $3.31 but I had to
catch my bus back home so
I gave him a quarter and some
pennies and told him to
read something for free
for the next person who came
along and he looked
like he thought that
would be a cool idea
so if some random
guy comes up to you
on the street speaking in
rhyming couplets you have
me to thank and if he
doesn't I guess the poem you just
read will have to do.

~ Kris Bluth

Corner of Willamette and Broadway

A statue of Ken Kesey sits
on a statue bench reading
a statue book to statue children.

Tweaker kids passing here.
Businessmen with
cigarettes passing there.

The locally-owned
donut shop fills the air.

A vacant lot becomes
office space while

Ken keeps telling his
statue story and in
another ten years all
those statue children
will be ten years older

someday.

~ Kris Bluth

Kris Bluth came to Eugene to attend the U of O and never left. His poems have most recently appeared in *Denali, Every Day Poets*, and *Groundwaters*.

EUGENE S. P. DEPOT - 1908

Autzen

At Autzen, audacious athletes attack
Before bellowing, brawling,
Cheering, caterwauling
Ducks, drinking in deafening decibels,
Endangering Eugenean's ears.
Frenetic football fans on
Game day, green, gold and giddy,
High on hash and Heineken's,
Indecently idolizing
Joes and Jacks,
Kick-off kings.
Louder and louder, like a
Million machine-guns,
Noise destroys the nerves and neurons,
Overwhelming opponents. Oregon
Passionately pushes and pulls to
Quell the enemy, quarter by quarter,
Ratcheting up the raucous rioting,
So stadium sounds surpass sonic booms on
Tarmac take-offs. Tumultuous tributes
Use up University
Vitality and voices,
Weakening waning
Xenophobic, X-rated
Yowls and yells at Aut-
Zen.

~ Jane Capron

Jane is a writer of mystery novels and belongs to the Osher Lifelong Learning Institute (OLLI) poetry group sponsored by the University of Oregon. A number of her novels, including *Hanky Panky* and *Best Friends* are set in Eugene.

Thirsty Thursday at Civic Stadium

draws crowds
Ems-fans – Lizzy Arthur
Rafael Niki Old Gus – emptying
just one more Bud-Light cupful cursing
the over-throw past third a Boise-boy crossing
home-plate so one more run gets tallied
on the scoreboard perched high
against the green South hills
and setting-sun   peanut-bags
hurled over head into fans' hands poised
to pass cash back in a split tennis-ball joke cheer
folks who drink up summer's heat
in concert neighbors belting out
old tunes full throttle sway
through the 7th-inning stretch: prep for more
farm-club drama—errors waiting to unfold as the night
gets old and tongues / arms / offers sway & swagger ever looser
leaning out suds / mitts / come-ons cupped
for a good-day's fair play / foul ball
locals filling the bleachers steady
as the unpredictable final score the mercury
bubbling wayward of ninety Thirsty-Thursdays
the Padres' farm club rocks old Civic Stadium bottom-
of-the-9th rallies—run by run hung by hand
the bleacher stomp deafening—rousing
every last South-Hills sleeper
the catcher's eye on the ball.

~ Deb Casey

Mammal, Up Top Pisgah

Across the frosted field wolf—moon high
in the branches last night
ages now this early
morning… getting
better at it I might agree
with my daughters: being human
vastly overrated—the coyote (first I've seen
on our hill) carries a wild-cat's ease, pack-dog's power
in its stride crossing my path with a grace I seek
practicing to keep knees and hips agile my own
gait easy as an upright warm-blooded
homo-sapien female past
middle age past
child-bearing breasts once belly heavy
with milk that nourished the children born
of my body live—squawky and ruddy, furry
early on—now sag, joints creaky,
placentas buried in tangles of root balls, trees
grown to bear their own fruit. Sweaty from the climb up
I watch coyote drop down Pisgah. Drawn toward
its uncompromised presence I inhale
the crispness. Hold our gaze.
Light of hoof / paw / foot
traversing the slope. No sound breaks the chill.
Contracting limbs and ambition I descend
the scrambly trail with a two-legged hiking friend.

~ Deb Casey

Deb Casey--with friends--has climbed Pisgah most every Tuesday for the last 18 years, & is perched on its hillside or river bank drawing weekly in fair weather. *AS-IS, Several Sisters* was recently published by Finishing Line Press.

Deliveries

I spent a few years, I don't know, maybe two
Delivering free books to the kids who lived
In the Downtown Eugene mall.
It made me feel better, I don't know, maybe
Because in every face I was looking for my brother
Maybe he lived in the Downtown Eugene Mall.
Once a week, I'd load up, go out and deliver
Cheap paperbacks to children too young to look so old
Constantly surprised by the tastes of those I served.
The young girl and the twenty-something man with her
I chose not to think about their relationship
Even when the straps of her tank top kept slipping down
She liked potboiler romance and young adult fiction
And he sometimes hovered around the edges
While she chose
Occasionally selecting a science fiction for him
Holding it out
Wings of hope in her face unfurling when he took it from her out-
    stretched hand
I gave a lot of books away
It got depressing when they were still there
In the rain
And my brother is still there, I think
I wonder if anyone brings him books?

~ Jennifer Chambers

Jennifer Chambers is the author of *Learning Life Again* and *Anna*, the first book of *The Curious Bookshop* series. She is an editor, writer and co-owner of *Groundwaters* Magazine and is a 2012 winner of the Erica Atkisson Memorial Scholarship Award.

The River is Fat Today

The River is fat today,
bloated by late melting snows,
roiling with runoff
from gray, rain-soaked May
that devoured Spring.

Unleashed, it rumbles
down the Valley's gut,
searching, seeking,
answering the mating call
of surf and sea.

Brave and bold,
lured by lunar lust,
it roars across the bar,
captured, cradled, rocked
between two shores.

Then teased aloft again,
enticed ashore, whipped to tears
and shattered shards of ice
it nestles among Cascade crests
and waits again the call of Spring.

~ Lee Darling

Lee Darling has been a resident of Oregon since 1961. She writes essays as well as poetry and published a novel, *Just Out of Reach*, in 2011.

Parade on Willamette Street. www.eugene-or.gov

Reluctant Coquette

Eugene in April's spring,
a cruel land of gray skies,
daily showers and icy pellets,
even snow to hide the drab.

Rare glimpse of sunshine tantalizes
with quick promise of warming rays,
scurries back to hide behind dark clouds
or the early night of days too short.

How like young maiden, a coquette
who breathes favors with dimpled smiles,
then quick away from eager swain
before his fevered hopes unmet.

The cold of winter lingers long.
No young lad I, tempted by hopes,
plaintive pleas, I yearn more from her,
more sun to warm my garden bed.

~ Gus Daum

Until recently, a writer of fiction and essays. In his mid-eighties, with the encouragement of Dr. Roy Johnston and *Groundwaters* Magazine, Gus embarked into poetry.

Eagles: For Ralph & Ingrid

Ralph,

Did you know that
this year
on Skinner's Butte
the bald eagles
have nested

Three handsome chicks
(so I hear)
easily visible

to the naked eye
(In fact, from her 6th floor
window, my student
looked up just as an eagle

swept by
within feet of the glass)

Ralph,

Last night
At the restaurant table
I saw Ingrid, her hand
like a wing on your shoulder
(how she holds you
in her heart)

Together you've written
and published, inspired
and taught

Parents together
Grandparents together

Our daughters together in school
All my years in Eugene
like high flying eagles
you two have graced
my personal sky

finally nesting
up close
— now we're friends —
I thank you for being

~ Joan Dobbie

Joan has been writing poetry since about 1975, steadily since around 1983. She has a 1988 M.F.A. in Creative Writing from the University of Oregon.

Tsunami Tsar

Eugene's Own Characters: Scott Landfield, owner of Tsunami Books

It's a famous place,
Tsunami Books,
— Ken Kesey read here,
shared his lusty spirit
with adoring crowds
who understood

One Slam Poet
— barely past her quarter-century mark —
encouraged this newbie
to risk all self-respect
at open mic for the first time
three years ago

"Always love to discover new poets,"
Jora LeFleur said
to my 60-year-old self
that memorable night
I read my limericks aloud

Her performance jazzed me
so much, I went home
and wrote a long one
 in her style

My poetry group meets here
sits high on this podium.
Scott loves us but frets
that our very presence
intimidates others
looking for that perfect collectible
on a shelf behind us
– serious poets –
cowered by our exuberance,
ricocheted ideas,
snatched inspiration,
atmospheric access
from the surging creativity
that surrounds us

He's a Eugene fixture,
Scott is,
loved by the town
doing what he wants
where he wants to be

but light years older than
that man who came
decades ago
in search of . . .
something more

like the town itself

~ Michele M. Graf

Michele is a poet, writer, editor, and creative mentor; her collaborative book of
poetry, *LIFELINES*, is available at Tsunami Books, and online. Join her adventure
at www.poetic-muselings.net.

Eugene, with Crows, March 2000

That year the planets were perfectly positioned
to deliver us here—this glacial field,
a wilderness of glass.

We found lions behind our rented duplex—
the English ivy was full of snakes
our cat hunted with utmost vigilance,

their bitten headless bodies
trailing from both sides of his mouth.
Now and then I'd save one,

fling it into the grass, watch as it slithered out
of sight. I stood mourning at the kitchen window,
my diminished life smoke curling around the curtains.

I wanted my mother, the daily round I'd left
three hours south, the unutterable
beauty of the familiar.

The crows, black slashes flaring in the March trees,
their sudden clacking ruckus. Each morning more crows came,
their wing-beats overhead the clapping of hands,

black outlines shoulder to shoulder on the telephone wire,
hunched against the relentless rain,
waiting for me to make my next move.

~ Toni Hanner
Originally Published in *West Wind Review*

Toni Hanner's poems appear in *Yellow Medicine Review, MARGIE, Alehouse, Calyx, Gargoyle, Tiger's Eye,* and others. She is a member of Lane Literary Guild's Red Sofa Poets and Port Townsend's Madrona Writers and published two books in 2012—*The Ravelling Braid from Tebot Bach*, and a chapbook of surrealist poems, *Gertrude, from Traprock*.

This Beautiful Spot Called Eugene

Here goes the blinding
beauty of new spring.
The colors run into
each other like the
smooth blanket
of morning fog
as it rolls from my mouth.

I have been told
by friends that
this fog can change
into another role,
that of a dark phantom.

My dear friend Toni
just relayed to me
the dark phantom she has
with depression,
and in France with Gods.

How do you kick back
in Eugene?
With such a veil,
light helps
so I'll stretch
that way.

~ Roy K. Johnston

Poet and musician Roy K. Johnston has been a featured reader at numerous international universities and festivals and his published books of poetry include *The System Is Broken; Seeds of Tolerance; Kenosis, San Luis Obispo; Dissonance and Consonance; The Wandering Circle.* For a more detailed biography, visit his website at http://roykjohnston.com.

EUGENE CITY HALL - 1915 TO 1964

22

The House Was Empty

The house was empty that first night –
after we crossed the northern tier in a Plymouth Voyager
stuffed with a cat, a Christmas tree, an eight- and a twelve-year old,
listening to Walkmans with their feet in the air, watching
movies on the Sony video player, through
Pennsylvania, Ohio, Indiana, Illinois, Iowa, Nebraska and South Dakota,

after we opened our gifts in a motel room in Wyoming
and ate cheese crackers and Doritos in a gas station,
because no restaurant was open on Christmas day,

after we chased the wagon trails through Idaho to Ontario,
Oregon, past the Strawberry Mountains, Painted Hills, Ochoco
Forest, the Three Sisters, and over Santiam Pass
and landed in Eugene.

with no moving truck in sight, we simply spread our
bodies in a parallelogram across the orange, shag,
wall-to-wall carpet in the living room
and began our new life.

~ Ruthy Kanagy

Ruthy is a poet, writer and bicycle travel consultant based in Eugene. She has a
poem in *Fault Lines Poetry Journal* and is the author of *Moon Living Abroad in Japan*.

Ascension
at Spencer's Butte

Head into clouds; climb mountains to find them,
before the rain hits, and you surrender yet
another day to these four walls and the
pretty little things you think keep you grounded.

Abandon your umbrella at the trailhead—
rid yourself of sky-blinders and ballast.
Hide your cell phone in the bushes with your
wallet and other identity tracers.

Set a brisk pace at the gate—get seizing.
It's not every day clouds settle within reach.
You'll find them just beyond the tree-line,
where wide open and sky's the limit get replaced

by uncertainty and mirrored ceilings.
Immerse yourself in open space until you get there,
look around, see how the birds see you: nothing
like a tree, yet rooted to the beaten path.

Combat your senses with sensation. There's a
feeling you're after like dunking your head
in a bucket of oblivion, like drowning
in now, like breathing eternity. Be.

You won't realize you're lost until you look
around and it's gone. Everything. Erased by clouds.
'Here' loses all relativity when you arrive. Now,
forget to breathe and lose your self completely.

Keep moving, trust your feet, set them in rhythm
with your heartbeat and listen to your mind.

It's always been there, right behind your eyes,
you've just been blinded by the busy-ness of life.

When you breach cloud cover at the crest, all that
exists is sunlight and blue sky; you're on an island
paradise adrift in a great, white ocean, no trace
of the world below—it feels like evolution.

Forget things left behind and listen to the birds;
they know what to do with freedom. Watch your
words flee like butterflies and disappear in the distance.
Don't chase them. You're right where you belong.

~ Jon Labrousse

A veteran of the Eugene Poetry Slam, Jon Labrousse has performed on almost
every stage in Eugene. When he's not teaching middle school, you can find him
on a bicycle, and/or in the woods, most likely with his two children.

Last Tuesday

Not a drop of rain fell the whole heavily-clouded
two-mile walk to the bakery where I was bound
to meet you at nine for breakfast pastries and
coffee, after empty weeks of not seeing you.
Who knew where the day would lead after we got
talking about, well, everything, but, especially,
adventure, something we often seek together,
which is why I carried that enormous umbrella
the whole damned way—first of all as a totem,
to hold back the rain, but also, just in case.

After breakfast by the fire in that Hideaway
place, we drove roundabout town in your
beat-up Subaru with the burnt-out brake-light
(the car whose timing belt you had replaced with your
own two hands—my heroine!), to negotiate
the best approach to your favorite tree in town.
We sat through three eventually green turn signals,
watching it partake of the rain until the honking behind
drove us back into the through lane in search
of a parking place near the river, just off campus.

We ended up parking behind that Thai place
off Franklin, under a two-hour sign, with just an
hour before you had to work the lunch shift across town
at another Thai place, which wasn't ironic at all.
It just meant we didn't have much time.
You stepped out of the car and lifted your face to the rain,
unworried about ruining your hair, or your
'who needs makeup?' So you'd walk closer to me, I did the
'chivalrous' thing and unleashed my ginormous blue
umbrella with its fashionable? yellow panels.

The thing was like a house, it shielded us not just
from the rain, but passersby, and when we settled
into one of the bench nooks on the footbridge
over the Willamette, I felt utterly alone
with you and the mated ducks we watched splash-landing
onto the swollen river, over and over again:
a couples' game they were playing, like dominoes.
There were small, calm pools in the rocks where other
duck-couples had settled, water rushing in rapids
around them. The hour boiled down to 60 seconds.

Back at your place, after racing across town, I waited
on the front-stoop while you changed, refrained from telling
you how beautiful you were, and had been all day,
when you emerged from the hallway, five minutes before
your shift, wanting to play hostess, show me the house.
I refused then, but I still want to be where you live.
We drove far too slowly down 28th, but made it
to the restaurant on time for your shift, and body-hugged
goodbye under the overhang at the backdoor
for what felt like an hour, but was definitely more.

When you called minutes later, I was wandering
backstreets home, wishing I had kissed you so much better
than that pulling away from the hug, polite smooch
at the corners thing. Kissed how I love your company,
kissed until we disappeared into each other
like chocolate milk. Wished I could do just that part,
the last part, over, when you called. "Hello?"
Work-shift canceled, you were already on your way
to the deli where we met for lunch. You grabbed me
by the raincoat and kissed me, 'Hello,' hard on the lips
before we went inside, so we wouldn't have to wait for goodbye.

~ Jon Labrousse

Hendricks Park

Mating dragonflies
Circling into the wind
Like a boomerang

Inside

Seven Months of Rain—
Jig-saw puzzles sold out
Eugene grows green

Rose Gardens

Early afternoon -
in lemony light I slept
leaning on a shrub

Albertson's Parking Lot

High on the wire
medley of Blackbirds, mothers
string of black pearls

Fern Ridge Rest Stop

Driving – daydreaming
flock of Blackbirds disoriented
a Hitchcock movie

~ Janine Margiotta

Wild Poppy

Passed by her
on the way home from the lake.
She sat on the side of the road,
torn denim jacket, jeans rolled
at the cuff, and barefoot.
Oblivious -
her back to the traffic.
Blistered thumb
   thumbing through
a magazine.
Not a care in the world;
except maybe about
what she was reading
or the wild orange poppy
delicately placed
   behind her ear.
She'll be hitching again by sun-down,
giving her thumb
time to peel, a sunburn
from being stretched out
too long
   in the sun.

~ Janine Margiotta
Originally published in *Groundwaters* Magazine, 2008

Janine Margiotta, a native of New York, tries to go back every other year to visit. When not writing, she and her six year old son Dylan like to skip rocks, hunt bugs and go to the park.

SHELTON - McMURPHEY HOME ON SKINNER'S BUTTE - 1898

Sonnet CCCVII (Eugene)

The sun burns through the fog upon the hill
The mist-bound firs splash color to the sky
A droplet casts a rainbow from my sill
As blackbirds from the lawn their breakfast pry
The warmth of morning's sun rides on the breeze
A deer devours a rose just up the street
A squirrel chirps his greeting from the trees
Upon a misty morning so complete.
The sound of traffic rises from below
A distant horn belies the lush terrain
Commuters watch a crane who's swooping low
To fish the ponds where nighttime mists have lain.
    Your fringes leave us glimpses of the wild
    While city lights delight the modern child.

~ Paul Stephen McCartney

Paul McCartney, the great grandson of a Scottish coal miner and a German farmer, is a retired school teacher with 72 years on earth and 45 of them in Eugene. He is a linguist and a geographer with two teens still living at home who are..."the sun and the moon of my life."

Now Boarding

I proceed quietly in queue to the plane's cabin door,
my new life... will soon take off.
New York to Oregon, all my dreams are
tightly packed in assorted luggage, contained in the plane's cargo
   compartment.
After searching the US for the perfect place to root,

I finally decided it must be Oregon.
Seeking diversity in all forms of life and cultures, I looked for a historic
   city
built by rugged pioneers, those that could forge a life, hammered by
   reason.
It had to be a small town residing within a city
that removes waste with more than one sort of recycling bin...
a city that feels like a village.

A grid where all cultures convene
all faiths that live together and look forward to assembling
in peace...
weather that never gets too cold, for too long...
and a fall that reveals all of her colors.

Mighty rivers that roar through the heart of that city... and
walkways that consider the needs of all ages.
Being able to hear all of nature's songs, above the sound of human
   congestion.
A place where small farms are invited to share and sell at Saturday's
   market.
Please fasten your seat belts for descent into...

with Mt. Hood and her sisters as my window's backdrop, we slow our
    descent over
a cratered valley, within an eagle's eye view of the Pacific Ocean.
I can almost smell the sweetness of air, from the fern and old-growth
    forests.
After a soft and effortless landing, we approach our arrival gate.
The cabin doors open to reveal her deep corridor.
Standing with hat in hand, a gate agent beams a toothy smile...

"Welcome Ma'am...

"Welcome to Eugene"

~ Barbara Newman

Barbara is a retired expatriate, living abroad in Orsa, Sweden and travels as often
as possible to visit a dear friend living in Eugene. She has had several poems
published in *Groundwaters* magazine in the past year.

Tsunami

A dying breed
that's shining bright
it's where we chill
at night.
Rough hewn boards
these timbers truss
and tea gratis
that's right.
Analogue rage
in this digital age,
chi and verse
backdrop the stage,
lick your fingers
turn the page.

Used bookstore score
Mary
Ferlinghetti
a Prechtel reading
at Tsunami.
Pick shelf print
is what we get
hometown respect
for this old-town gent.

~ cameron parker

cameron parker is a writer, artist, and founder of the *Watercourse Journal* (www.watercoursejournal.com). He lives and works in the Willamette Valley, Oregon with his wife and three sons.

Memories Along the Oregon Trail

Our grandmothers told the stories of their grandmothers
of sod houses built in a lonely prairie at the end of a long trail,
of cooking gathered berries and roots and harvested grains
over open fires in sodded firepits.

we mourn the loss of the oral tales
to the reading of books of other's stories
and to the modern magic of movies and television
we mourn the loss of our own story,

but our history is there among our fractured families
in bits and pieces scattered and forgotten,
yet we feel we know it and know we could tell it again
if we could but call forth that distant past
from our buried genetic memory.

today we pitch our domed tents in a forest campsite,
tell ghost stories, sing songs, share bits of memories
we suddenly remember from grandmother's tales
and feel again the old magic of storytelling.

we cook a huckleberry cobbler — perhaps grandmother's recipe —
made with berries we picked ourselves along the hiking trail
bake it in a dutch oven over an open campfire in a sodded firepit
    . . . our grandmothers watching over our shoulders
    . . . perhaps.

~ Eileen Dawson Peterson

Ms. Peterson has been writing poetry since 1948 and was first published in
Young America Sings and *Songs of Youth* Anthologies in 1953.

Villard Hall on the campus of the University of Oregon;
en.wikipedia.org/wiki/File:VillardHall.jpg

Eugene

It's appeared on the list of Top Ten Towns.
If we still had town criers doing their rounds
they'd be touting it as a great place to live
(despite the grief grass seed pollen can give).

We've an array of ART forms up the wazoo:
a Bach Festival, Tsunami Slams, the Bijou
and graphic art galleries plus the Schnitzer.
To Katmandu, Nepal: a twin-city sister.

Most nights you can pop in to see a live play
at the Leebrick, V.L.T., Hult or Cabaret.
Number one on the list of cities that are GREEN,
Saturday Market'll sell you a fresh string-bean.

A fine college and a top university
can add to what you learned at your mama's knee.
The whole town turns to bright yellow and green
when a big sports event grabs the Autzen scene.

Catch the Eugene Celebration's Pet Parade,
or some fancy-type brew that beats lemonade.
Pick up the *Eugene Weekly* for free on Thursday.
A ski resort's less than a day's drive away.

Music clubs, that rock, can be heard for miles.
This berg often hosts Olympic-style trials,
is where cyclists are kings and Nike has a role
and was once aptly known as "Skinner's Mud-hole."

This city that's named after Skinner, Eugene,
just like New York, has its own magazine.

~ Jean Marie Purcell

Jean Marie used to teach kids and is currently trying her hand at playwriting...
"I'm a perpetual dieter."

The Ghost of Patchouli Past

What is that scent,
Reminding me of
Momma's Homefried Truckstop?

Tie-died T-shirts,
Long hair,
Birkenstocks with wool socks,
Velvet vests embroidered in tiny mirrors,
Wrap-skirts from India
And bare feet with ankle bracelets.

I can even smell buckwheat pancakes
With organic maple syrup.
Alonzo wears bloomers and fez,
While I'm in my dashiki.
Our fiddle duets waft over the crowd,
As we play for breakfast and tips.

That's strong coffee, man!

~ Rachel Rich

McKenzie Baptism

I plunge into the river,
Like a sinner about to be reborn
And emerge refreshed, renewed,
Glad to be alive.

Aware only of this body;
No thoughts, no worries.
Inner heat resists cold,
Feet recoil from jagged rocks.

I rise to the surface,
Stroking water first urgently,
Then with confidence –
Bathing in liquid summer.

~ Rachel Rich
Originally published in *Groundwaters* Magazine, 2009

Weaving together micro with macro, Rachel Rich draws images from nature, travel and relationships. Her work appears in *Groundwaters*, as well as the chapbooks *Payne's Gray* and *Shadowlines* available at Tsunami Books.

Aphrodite Has Had It

up to here with all the skinny girls
boosting their cleavage and showing off,
as if Zeus and the others need any
more encouragement. No, the Queen
of Love isn't getting enough lately,
Ares always marshalling the boys at Serbu
and Hephaestus blacksmithing for Ninkasi,
so she's as green-eyed as Hera

when Psyche saunters by on the downtown mall,
ripped fishnets under short-shorts, black
leather bustier and gobs of dark makeup.
All of 13, the goddess thinks, and flies
to her son Eros's cabin in the high Cascades.
She tells him to fix it with his arrows
"so the girl falls for the next droopy-drawered
dreadlocked wannabe Rasta to shamble by,
showered or not."

Eros, he's no mama's boy. "Look, Venus,"
he drawls, pissing her off with her Roman name.
"You're totally out of touch up there
in the South Hills. Down on Blair girls
like that are all over the place. She's
just trying to fit in, pretty as she is."

An angry gull, Aphrodite beats her wings
and screams, "I'll show that floozy 'pretty'!"
But Eros cuts her off. "Ma, don't worry.
Dudes don't pay attention. They're workin'
their GameBoys like we used to goof around
with those Olympic rings Heph always made.
Listen, I'm not shootin' any arrows.
You're still the prettiest goddess in town."

Such a crooner, and she almost buys it
on her way back to Skyline Blvd.
But, Aphrodite's no loser. She banks left
and heads for the mall. She knows
her devious, backtalking god of a son
has packed his quiver and flown to Eugene,
thinking that hottie, Psyche, might still be around.
Aphrodite will always ensure
Eros shoots his arrows right.

~ Jenny Root

Jenny Root has published poems in several literary journals including *basalt*,
Windfall, *Hipfish*, and *Fault Lines* and work is forthcoming in *Cloudbank* and *Edge*.
Her work is anthologized in *What the River Brings* and *New Poets of the American
West*.

Plum Wine

I heard you planted trees for a living once
slowly paying off the old house on 7th Street
paint peeled off the door, bare boards.
That night, the guitar in your hands
jamming with a reggae woman
on stage at the Coffee Bean
your offering was plum wine
learning riffs, trading them for plum blossoms.

Now I'm lying on the grassy hill, looking up
clouds move apart in the sky, the sun
warms my face as I think about that evening
your voice a little raspy
an era has ended.

~ Janice D. Rubin

Janice Rubin is a poet, counselor & educator. Her chapbook, *Transcending Damnation Creek Trail & other Poems*, was published by Flutter Press in 2010.

Northwestern

i sit and wait, beside the bronze statue
of Eugene Skinner, founder of this town,
drunk on words and half a plastic glass
of red wine. his profile is pensive,
his boots heavy, wide-brimmed hat
in hand. the air thick with an after
glow of rain. damp trails wind down
from my pen into northwestern earth.

~ Jemila Nurjehan Spain

Jemila Nurjehan Spain loves words, movement, and spirituality in all forms. She is deeply grateful to the many wonderful friends in her life, and to the natural world for being a continual source of comfort and guidance.

Gulls & Crows

All along the bike paths of our town, crows
lord-around in trees, making caustic comments we sort of understand;
or they row majestically through open skies
    — and we assume
they're in charge of certain things.

Once, they were part of a very old story,
    spoken   s-l-o-w-l-y
    chanted   s-l-o-w-l-y
as a song in winter, in rain,
for an audience who really knew its birds.

But I want to tell you
something new about the story:

The crows in this town are more numerous than the gulls.
The gulls in this town are larger than the crows.

Come with me and stand by a field
between the middle school
and the millrace. Watch
how the gulls waddle in scads like ducks.

These gulls are amassing for a reason.

44

Our parks belong to the crows, but meanwhile
the gulls are staking out the lesser fields;
for months, maybe longer, they've been
passing themselves off
as somewhat overweight pigeons.
Sure, they look pale, sluggish and harmless
especially to the crows, who probably think
they *are* pigeons.
   But lately
there are more and more and more of them about.

Something is cooking. A war of turf and claw,
of wing and craw. Any day now, they'll be out
on the track field, massing in rows, for
The Battle of Gulls and Crows, an ancient contest
to be re-enacted in our very city, among our fields
and streams, our sidewalks and trees.
The pigeons are selling tickets already.

~ Anita Sullivan

Anita Sullivan is a retired piano tuner who has published a couple of poetry collections with local publishers (Traprock Books and Airlie Press). She is active in the Eugene-Springfield literary community.

Garden One on A Garden Tour

Katsura trees, Asian pears, older plum plants
and an atoll of blueberry bushes. Purple waving foxgloves
and violet pansy and futon resting on the back deck.

Purple was blowing, inflecting in art, skirt, blouse or plant.
Purple is the color of wit, intelligence, knowledge, devotion and a
common color of the day and the common Katsura tree.

A Gigantic Beech in Late June
A Garden Tour of the Mayor's Garden and The Whiteaker District

A Zimbabwe calabash resonator, deze, hums
thrice from the local musicians Jerome and Joel
sitting under the big English Beech and these pipers
on an amplifier, a resonator, a rhythm instrument
follow us garden visitors out the path
from the mayor's home on this tour.

Ferns and starts from vegetable cages
surround the welcoming knotted beech tree,
a good place for summer music reading as the name
derived from several languages: Buch in German, in Sweden,
the word of book, and Boc in Old English and Bok in Old Norse.
This beech spans three neighbor's homes and three planting zones.

Smoky hums welcome their use in smoky beers,
cheeses and some drum making from the beech as
this is a thumb drum in a gourd.

~ Nicole Taylor

Nicole is an artist, a hiker, a poetry note taker, a sketcher, a volunteer, and a
dancer, formerly in Salem's DanceAbility. She has been accepted at several print
and online publications and she blogs at apoetessanthology.blogspot.com.

Eugene, on a Thin-Clouded Night

Exiting the revolving doors of the mall
empty-handed, she's drawn off-course
by flute notes curling inside her dried stems
of hope, long notes pulling slow
as the Willamette's current.

Bats flicking through park trees, the bones
of her past reaches ready for a kiln,
she imagines her soul as a vase
again waiting for rose stems.

Sounds from current and traffic pyramid
in his soul as he stands midway
on the pedestrian bridge with various
characters waiting for moonrise.

Another long note requiems down
among the cairns built in shallows on
a too hot day, his flute singing to a river
and those long-faced into years of sifting

through loss. Moon rising, gray-blue halo
on the centrifuge of this thin-clouded night.
Gray-blue glints riding the wave-crests
like petals rippling into the ocean
as the fog mare canters in on the waves.

~ Charles Thielman

Charles Thielman was raised in Charleston, S.C. and Chicago, educated at red-bricked universities and on city streets. Charles was married on a Kauai beach in 2011 and is a loving grandfather of five free spirits.

Deady Hall, UO Campus; en.wikipedia.org/wiki/Deady_Hall

Grounded

Bark grew on trees before I moved to Eugene.
In Eugene, bark grows in people's yards
a ground cover shredded onto black plastic.
It grows in landscaping trucks that vend along the streets.
It grows in piles along trails to be
and it grows beneath the feet
of runners along the Amazon Canal,
runners who run a winding mile
around and around and around.
Summer bark dust stains their shoes
puffs up behind each pounding foot
fills the lungs of the next
around and around and around.
In winter the trail squishes.
Winter to spring
and slowly camas lilies rise blue
around and around.
But they bloom unseen
and the runners miss the totem pole
   held by a rope
near the third-quarter mile marker
and the runners miss the mallards
   courting on the water
and the runners miss the green heron cruising
   and the blue heron stalking
and the crows flying to roost
   in the ash grove at dusk.
The runners stop-watching, sweat-watching,
   breath-watching, muscle-stretching,
bark-watching, around.

~ Susanne Twight-Alexander

Susanne has lived in Eugene since 1989 after 25 years of living in Trinity County in Northern California where her three children were born. An avid hiker/photographer (and occasional participant in 5Ks), she has recently published her first book of poems, *Being*.

49

Ev'ryone's An Artist

Graffitti, then, all over Eugene,
on alleyway fences,
on the backside of industrial buildings,
here, and no surprise, there.

But it's all relative, for upon entering Milan
by bus, graffitti is spray-canned everywhere
to the height of one's shoulders
upon all the storefront buildings.

And check out the railway
into Frankfurt's city center
via the U-Bahn or especially
the local U-Drei.
Grafitti! All along the route,
suburban to urban,
and again it's as high as the spray can reach,
signaling the disaffection of youth,
the need to say in so many puffs,
that the young killroys were here.

But then, amble down to
Eugene's Whiteaker neighborhood,
along the Union Pacific tracks,
and find a cement block wall
just dedicated to the artists
who may never have even heard
of Banksy, or his mad French acolyte.

So, youngsters, paint your visions
upon that wall, make your mark
and proclaim your artistry
in broad daylight, or evening's
tranquil glow, in an
array of hues.

It's there for the taking, that public space,
an alternative to the underpass
along the Slough, where
a dedicated citizen
blanks over all your work
in shades of battleship gray,
a true republican who works
with donated paint, in all weathers.

Eugene's dedicated space, along the railroad tracks,
is a democratic invitation
to make one's art
with no judgment from the elders
except to say, well maybe
that cerulean blue
could have profited
from a touch of green,
or that filigree there, I don't know,
it needs some understated orange...

And meanwhile, all those freight cars
roaring through, with all their signal statements
expressed but for an eye blink,
they're so ephemeral, while you stand grounded,
here in Eugene, with your art for the ages.

~ Tim Volem

Tim Volem writes poems for diversion and from necessity. He has been published
in *English Journal, Tiger's Eye* and *Carapace* and has a poem recently published in
Tribute to Orpheus 2.

As If

Condon Elementary School

A swift two
or three flitting over
the abandoned school then more plunging into the chimney

a blurry funnel
their chee and chirring overhead
a multitude scattered across the sky it's their coming back

that gets us
the air trembling troubled as memory
whistling satiny feathers arranging and rearranging in the dark

cramped shaft
over the dead furnace birds
hurrying down now like smoke billowing back into the chimney

as if smoke
could return to its fire
the wood to its tree in the sun on the hill as if flesh returned

wheeled back
through the locks and chambers
back into its clothes onto the crowded train backing away.

~ John Witte
Originally published in *The Hurtling*, Orchises Press, 2005

John Witte is the author of three poetry collections, including *Second Nature*, selected by Linda Bierds for the Pacific Northwest Poetry Series of the University of Washington Press. The recipient of numerous fellowships and awards, Witte lives with his family in Eugene, Oregon, where he teaches ecopoetry and literature courses at the University of Oregon.

Death Hat

About John Kovtynovich, the first resident on our hillside in
Southeast Eugene, an unforgettable character, and scion.

What if not
a flame on his head did you see him
striding down the road the deer bounding away old Kovtynovich

in such a hat
purple scarlet lime or was it
just the evening light maybe he grabbed whatever was at hand

his being
cold and in a hurry swinging
his arms like a young man with pollen and flowers in his hair

orchids dahlias
how could this be him so serious
an engineer he knows his struts and spans his works the water

gurgling through
the culvert under the road a stream
swerving under him through the gleaming corrugations who said

he was passing away
down to fluids he was shrinking
his bedroom filling with people who were they and what about

his apples and
what is he doing out and where
on earth is he going in such a lavish hat and why the smile

~ John Witte
Originally published in *The Hurtling*, Orchises Press, 2005

Contact:

C. Steven Blue, Publisher/Editor, Arrowcloud Press
cstevenblue@hotmail.com
www.wordsongs.com

Pat Edwards, Managing Editor, *Groundwaters* magazine
P.O. Box 50, Lorane, OR 97451 or
contact@groundwaterspublishing.com
www.groundwaterspublishing.com